Carnival Readers

The Car and the Donkey Cart

General editors
L. M. Arnold and Alice E. Varty

© Copyright text The Macmillan Press Ltd 1977, 1994
© Copyright illustrations The Macmillan Press Ltd 1994

All rights reserved. No reproduction, copy or transmission of this publication may be made without written permission.

No paragraph of this publication may be reproduced, copied or transmitted save with written permission or in accordance with the provisions of the Copyright, Designs and Patents Act 1988, or under the terms of any licence permitting limited copying issued by the Copyright Licensing Agency, 90 Tottenham Court Road, London W1P 9HE.

Any person who does any unauthorised act in relation to this publication may be liable to criminal prosecution and civil claims for damages.

First published 1977 as *The Car and the Bullock Cart*
Reprinted 1991
This edition published 1994

Published by THE MACMILLAN PRESS LTD
London and Basingstoke
Associated companies and representatives in Accra, Auckland, Delhi, Dublin, Gaborone, Hamburg, Harare, Hong Kong, Kuala Lumpur, Lagos, Manzini, Melbourne, Mexico City, Nairobi, New York, Singapore, Tokyo.

ISBN 0-333-61808-4

Printed in Egypt by Elias Modern Press

A catalogue record for this book is available from the British Library.

Illustrations by *Jenny Norton*

A man had a lovely red car. The car went very fast. The man talked about his lovely red car all the time.

Everyone was tired of his talk. "Let's have a race," they said. "Let's find a faster car to win the race." But nobody had a faster car.

"Let's get a bus," someone said.
But the buses were too big, they did not go very fast. They were slower than the lovely red car.

"Let's get a train," someone said.
But the train could not go on the road.
"Can nothing race the man's red car?"
everyone said.

A donkey and a donkey cart stood in the road. The driver was asleep in the cart. "Let me race the car," the donkey said.

Everyone laughed.
"You!" they said. "The car can go twenty times faster than you can. Don't be foolish! Anyway, your driver is asleep."

"Let him sleep!" said the donkey. "I know where to go."

Everyone laughed again.

Six small boys stood near the cart.
"Come and race the car!" said the six small boys to the donkey.

The six small boys spoke to the man with the lovely red car.
"The donkey is going to race your car," they said. "Come and race the donkey and his cart."

The man with the car laughed and laughed.
"What a foolish donkey!" he said. "How can he win a race with my fast red car? But come on. Let's have a race for ten miles. I am going to teach the donkey that he can't win a race with my lovely fast car."

Someone said, "One, two, three, go!" and the car went off.
The driver of the donkey cart was still asleep, but the donkey walked down the road.

The six small boys cried, "Faster, faster!"
They all ran after the cart.
"Come on, come on, faster!" they called to the donkey.
And the donkey walked down the road.

The car went for two miles, then the man in the car was thirsty.
"The donkey can't catch me," he said.
"I am going to stop and get a drink."
He stopped at a house to get a drink of water.

He stopped for a long time at the house. Then he saw the donkey cart coming down the road. He said, "I am going to go now."
He got into his car again and went on.

The donkey walked down the road.

The car went another three miles, then the driver was hungry.
"The donkey can't catch me," he said.
"I am going to get something to eat."

He stopped at a friend's house to get something to eat. He stopped a long time at the house.
He talked and laughed with his friend.

And the donkey walked down the road.

At last the man saw the donkey cart coming down the road and he said, "I am going to go now."
He got into his car and went on.

The car went for another four miles. Then the driver was tired.
"The donkey can't catch me," he said.
"I am going to sleep."

He stopped the car under a tree and went to sleep. He slept for a long, long time.
And the donkey walked down the road.

"Faster, faster!" said the six small boys.
They still ran beside the cart.
"Come on, come on, faster!" they called
to the donkey.
And the donkey walked down the road.

The donkey passed the car and walked on down the road. The driver of the donkey cart and the driver of the lovely red car were still asleep.

Soon the donkey saw the finishing line.
Everyone was there to see who won.

They saw the donkey cart coming first, and they all laughed.
"Hurray!" they said. "Come on donkey, come on!"

And the donkey walked down the road and won the race.

The car driver woke up and saw that it was late.
He saw the sunset behind the hills.

He drove very fast to catch the donkey, but he did not win the race. He was asleep for too long.

"I went to sleep. That is why you won the race," said the car driver to the donkey.

"My driver was asleep all the time," said the donkey. "I can win a race without a driver."

Then the driver of the donkey cart woke up and everyone shouted and laughed. "Your donkey won the race," shouted the six small boys. They walked down the road.

But the man with the car drove away.
He went home and he never talked about
his lovely red car again.

Words to learn for this book

donkey   cart   race   sunset
thirsty   tired   finishing line

Reading comprehension questions

1. What did the man talk about all the time?
2. Why did everyone laugh when the donkey said he was going to race the car?
3. How long was the race?
4. What happened when the six small boys cried, "Faster, faster!"?
5. Why did the man stop after two miles?
6. What did the man do at his friend's house?
7. Why did the man decide to go to sleep?
8. Why was everyone at the finishing line?
9. Why couldn't the driver catch the donkey?
10. What did the six small boys tell the driver of the donkey cart?